D1237826

SCIENCE STARTERS

Light

by Carolyn Bernhardt

BLASTOFF!
3
READERS

BELLWETHER MEDIA • MINNEAPOLIS, MN

Note to Librarians, Teachers, and Parents:

Blastoff! Readers are carefully developed by literacy experts and combine standards-based content with developmentally appropriate text.

Level 1 provides the most support through repetition of high-frequency words, light text, predictable sentence patterns, and strong visual support.

Level 2 offers early readers a bit more challenge through varied simple sentences, increased text load, and less repetition of high-frequency words.

Level 3 advances early-fluent readers toward fluency through increased text and concept load, less reliance on visuals, longer sentences, and more literary language.

Level 4 builds reading stamina by providing more text per page, increased use of punctuation, greater variation in sentence patterns, and increasingly challenging vocabulary.

Level 5 encourages children to move from "learning to read" to "reading to learn" by providing even more text, varied writing styles, and less familiar topics.

Whichever book is right for your reader, Blastoff! Readers are the perfect books to build confidence and encourage a love of reading that will last a lifetime!

This edition first published in 2019 by Bellwether Media, Inc.

No part of this publication may be reproduced in whole or in part without written permission of the publisher. For information regarding permission, write to Bellwether Media, Inc., Attention: Permissions Department, 6012 Blue Circle Drive, Minnetonka, MN 55343.

Library of Congress Cataloging-in-Publication Data

Names: Bernhardt, Carolyn, author.
Title: Light / by Carolyn Bernhardt.
Description: Minneapolis, MN : Bellwether Media, Inc., 2019. | Series: Blastoff! Readers. Science Starters
| Includes bibliographical references and index. | Audience: 5-8. | Audience: K to 3.
Identifiers: LCCN 2017061625 (print) | LCCN 2018009247 (ebook) | ISBN 9781681035413 (ebook)
| ISBN 9781626178083 (hardcover ; alk. paper) | ISBN 9781618914644 (pbk. ; alk. paper)
Subjects: LCSH: Light–Juvenile literature.
Classification: LCC QC360 (ebook) | LCC QC360 .B53 2019 (print) | DDC 535–dc23
LC record available at https://lccn.loc.gov/2017061625

Editor: Christina Leaf   Designer: Josh Brink

Printed in the United States of America, North Mankato, MN

Table of
Contents

Light Is Everywhere!

You are camping with your family. As the sun sets, faces glow in the campfire's light. Far off, the moon shines on the lake's **surface**.

Later, your flashlight guides you to your tent. All these lights make camping possible!

What Is Light?

Light is all around us! It bounces off of things and reaches our eyes so we can see.

It comes from **light sources** such as the sun and **electric** lamps.

Light is made up of **particles** of **energy** that are too small for us to see. They move in waves.

Light **reflects** off of objects. It hits something at an **angle** and bounces back at the same angle.

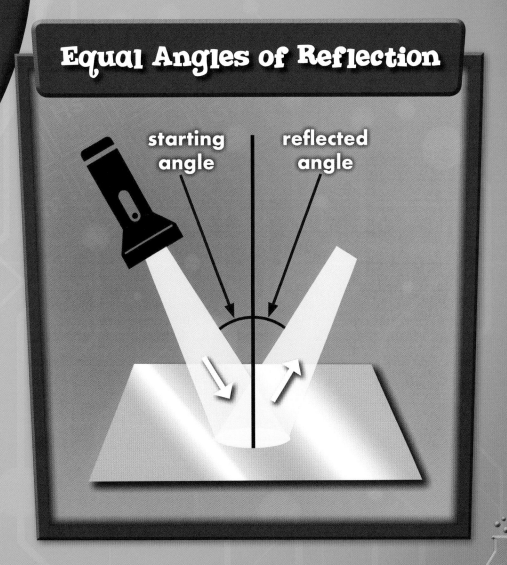

Equal Angles of Reflection

starting angle

reflected angle

Light and Color

Light's waves can have different **wavelengths**. This makes color! Longer wavelengths make reds and oranges. Shorter wavelengths make purples and blues.

Wavelengths and Color

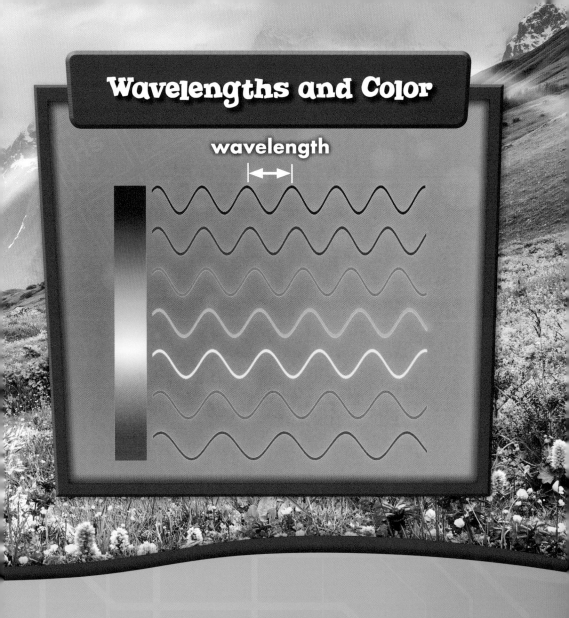

wavelength

When all wavelengths mix together, it makes white light. Sunlight is made of white light.

Objects get their color from either **absorbing** or reflecting certain wavelengths. Most objects absorb one or more colors.

If we see a blue ball, it means the ball reflects blue light. All other colors get absorbed.

Some objects reflect all light.
This makes them look white.

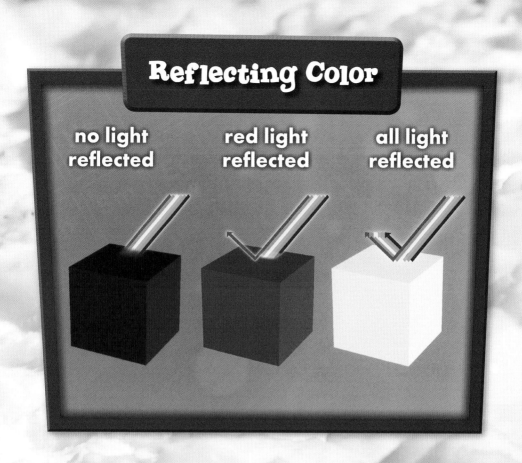

Reflecting Color

no light reflected **red light reflected** **all light reflected**

Other objects reflect no light. Instead, they absorb it all. These objects look black.

Shadows

shadow

Objects that block light's path cast shadows. Some objects, such as rocks, block all light. They make dark shadows.

Other objects, such as glass bottles, create lighter shadows because they let some light through.

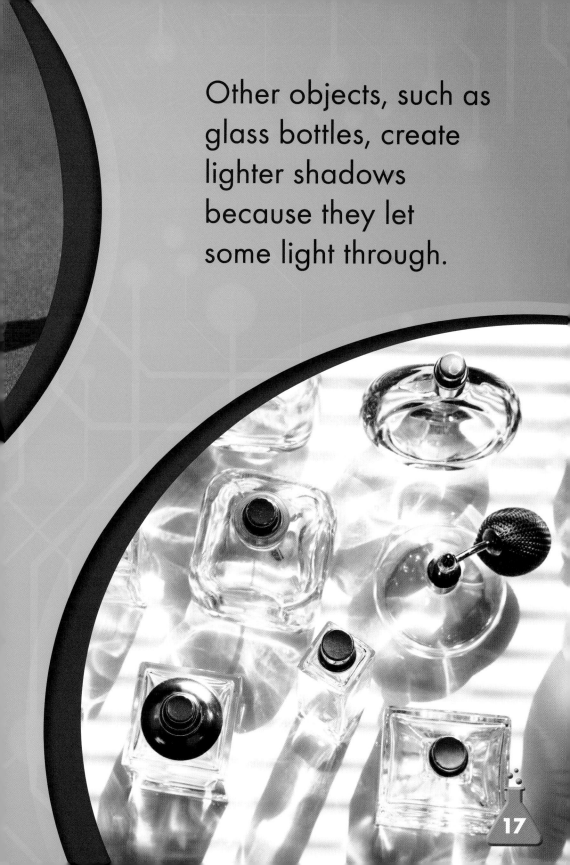

Shadows change as the sun moves across the sky during the day. The sunlight strikes objects at different angles. This changes the size of shadows all around you!

Measuring Shadows

You can see for yourself how light changes shadows!

What you will need:

- a clear plastic food container
- a rock
- chalk

1. Find some space on a sidewalk or driveway.
2. Go out early in the morning and put your container and your rock on the pavement.
3. Trace the objects' shadows in chalk on the pavement.
4. Go back to your objects in the afternoon. Trace your objects' shadows again. Are they longer or shorter?
5. Trace your objects' shadows one last time just before the sun sets. Do you notice anything different?
6. Compare the length, shape, and look of the shadows. Did you see a difference in the kind of shadow the container cast and the kind of shadow the rock cast?

Light on Earth

The sun is Earth's main **source** of light. Energy from the sun keeps our plants alive. This gives us food, which then gives us energy.

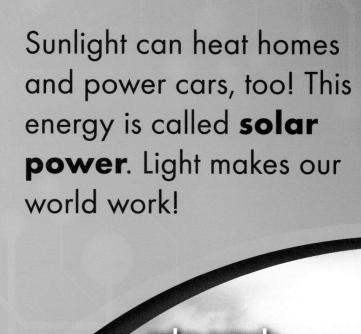

Sunlight can heat homes and power cars, too! This energy is called **solar power**. Light makes our world work!

solar panels

Glossary

absorbing—taking in or soaking up

angle—the shape formed when two lines meet

electric—something that runs on electricity; electricity is a form of energy that travels through wires and is used to operate machines and lights.

energy—useable power that allows things to be active

light sources—things that create light

particles—tiny amounts of something

reflects—bounces back waves of light, sound, or heat

solar power—power made by using the energy of the sun's rays

source—where something starts or comes from

surface—an outside part or layer of something

wavelengths—the distances between two peaks in a wave of energy

To Learn More

AT THE LIBRARY

Claybourne, Anna. *Light and Dark*. Minneapolis, Minn.: Lerner Publishing, 2016.

Kuskowski, Alex. *Science Experiments with Light*. Minneapolis, Minn.: ABDO Pub. Co., 2014.

Pfeffer, Wendy. *Light is All Around Us*. New York, N.Y.: Harper, 2014.

ON THE WEB

Learning more about light is as easy as 1, 2, 3.

1. Go to www.factsurfer.com.

2. Enter "light" into the search box.

3. Click the "Surf" button and you will see a list of related web sites.

With factsurfer.com, finding more information is just a click away.

Index

The images in this book are reproduced through the courtesy of: charobnica, front cover (periodic table); John Dakapu, front cover (circuit); ktsdesign, front cover (hero); Sharfsinn, p. 4; Stas Tolstnev, p. 5; Serhii Yurkiv, p. 6; bbernard, p. 7; Bildagentur Zoonar GmbH, p. 8; ilicon, p. 9; Kotenko Oleksandr, pp. 10-11; EVAfotografie, p. 12; wavebreakmedia, p. 13; FotoRequest, pp. 14-15, DCrane, p. 16; images and videos, p. 17; Yongyut Kumsri, p. 18; Tamara JM Peterson, p. 19; Nuttawut Uttamaharad, p. 20; SusaZoom, p. 21, oksana 2010, p. 24.

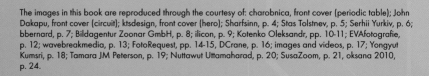